The HOME is BEST Book

by KATHLEEN N. DALY

Pictures by JAN PFLOOG

formerly **THE NEST BOOK**

 GOLDEN PRESS
Western Publishing Company, Inc.
Racine, Wisconsin

© 1968, 1976 by Western Publishing Company, Inc.
All rights reserved. Produced in U.S.A.

Second Printing, 1977

East, West, home is best—
sometimes home's a hanging nest.

A cave is home to big, black Bear.

A cozy den is Fox's lair.

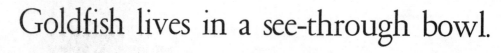

Goldfish lives in a see-through bowl.

Mousie lives in a deep, warm hole.

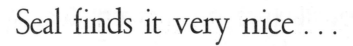

Seal finds it very nice ...

. . . swimming under northern ice.

The barn is home to gentle Cow.

Squirrel lives high up on a bough.

Dog's at home in his own snug house.

Martins have an apartment house.

Raccoon lives in a hollow tree.

And Pussycat lives here—with me.